MW01016140

The Lostness
of Mankind

The Lostness of Mankind

ONE MOTIVATION FOR EVANGELISM

By Louis L. King

Copyright © 1991 by Christian Publications
Camp Hill, Pennsylvania

ISBN: 0-87509-449-X

Printed in the United States of America

CHRISTIAN PUBLICATIONS
Camp Hill, Pennsylvania 17011

Foreword

I t is becoming increasingly difficult to take a firm theological stand on the slippery slope of religious pluralism in the Western world. But in this compact treatise on the most critical theological issue of this century, Louis L. King has taken a stand squarely on the clarity of Scripture as it relates to the eternal destiny of all people.

He has done it in his characteristic style—thorough, clear and without compromise. His discerning resistance to the multicultural milieu, the attractive appeal to impeccable human logic and the growing peer pressure of high profile evangelical theologians makes him a prophetic voice at the end of this, the greatest missionary century.

Dr. Arnold L. Cook
Vice President, Personnel and Missions
The Christian and Missionary Alliance in Canada

The Lostness of Mankind

ONE MOTIVATION
FOR EVANGELISM

By Louis L. King
Past President, The Christian and
Missionary Alliance

I t is common for evangelicals to say that evangelism and missions are necessary because people without Christ are lost. We engage in evangelism to rescue them, to save them. Among evangelicals, however, there is a general inability to describe the present, intermediate and resurrection states of the lost. With divine help and recourse to God's Word, I purpose to clarify these points.

I. The Source of Our Knowledge of Mankind's Lostness

Our knowledge of people's lostness if they are outside of Christ is derived exclusively from the Bible. Philosophy does not help us. This knowledge cannot be learned by reasoning or by research. It cannot be established inductively or deductively. God Himself reveals the fact in His Word. It is an article of *faith*. We perceive it only by divine enlightenment.

People's lostness is Spirit-taught truth which those untuned to the Spirit cannot receive (1 Corinthians 2:14). Their darkened understanding is not capable of this awareness by their own reasoning powers (Ephesians 4:18). This knowledge comes only

1

through revelation. Indeed, everything of a spiritual nature depends upon the Supreme Revelator, Jesus Christ. What we believe about Him, who He is and what He teaches will ultimately determine how we regard our fellow beings who do not share in our knowledge of Jesus.

Who, then, is Jesus Christ? The apostle John writes:

> *The Word became flesh and made his dwelling among us. We have seen his glory, the glory of the One and Only, who came from the Father, full of grace and truth.* John 1:14

> *Grace and truth came through Jesus Christ.* John 1:17b

Jesus Himself declared:

> *I am the way and the truth and the life.* John 14:6a

From these three texts we learn that Jesus Christ is the truth, that He is full of truth and that He brings truth to us.

The King of Truth, Jesus Christ, taught the Bible's divine inspiration, its impregnable truth and its complete authority. He declared of the Old Testament Law, "Until heaven and earth disappear, not the smallest letter, not the least stroke of a pen, will by any means disappear from the Law" (Matthew 5:18). Later He rebuked two of His followers for not believing "all that the prophets [had] spoken" (Luke 24:25). In a confrontation with some of His fellow Jews, Jesus emphasized that "the Scripture cannot be broken" (John 10:35).

Kenneth B. Kantzer, former editor of *Christianity Today,* writing in *The Church's Worldwide Mission,* has said of those statements:

> This testimony of Jesus Christ validates directly the Old Testament, but indirectly it

2

includes the New Testament as well. Our Lord constituted His disciples as His witnesses who should follow Him. He promised to guide them into all truth (John 16:13). He assured them of confirming signs of their apostolic authority in predictive prophecy and miracles. After His death and resurrection, His apostles claimed to represent their Lord and to have the right to speak with authority in the Church of Christ (Galatians 1-2). Their claims were confirmed by diverse miracles and gifts of the Holy Spirit (Hebrews 2:4).[1]

Since the question of people's lostness outside of Christ is an article of biblical faith, we go back to the basic question: "What do we think about Christ?" Do we accept Him as the King of Truth? Do we accept His position on the inspiration and authority of Scripture?

If we do accept Jesus as Truth, to be consistent we must accept and submit to His teachings and those of the fully attested Word on this so-important subject of mankind's lostness. If we acknowledge Jesus Christ as Savior, Lord and *Truth,* we must accept the Scriptures He enjoined upon us. They are the means we have of learning the Lord's will. Furthermore, His teachings have complete, final and binding authority over us as His disciples.

Conversely, to ostensibly accept Christ as sovereign Lord and Supreme Teacher and at the same time reject what He says about the Bible and about mankind's lost condition is grossly inconsistent. Indeed, to quote William G.T. Shedd:

> The strongest support of the doctrine of endless punishment is the teaching of Christ, the Redeemer of Man. . . . Jesus is the person who is responsible for the doctrine of eternal perdition. He is the

Being with whom all opponents of this
theological tenet are in conflict.[2]

We must accept, therefore, the Bible's presentation
of man's condition without reservation. We must
require no other validation. On the basis that Jesus is
Lord and Truth, we must accept the Bible as our
only but completely authoritative and trustworthy
source of knowledge about people's spiritual
condition.

II. The Present State of People without Christ

Jesus likened lost people to a lost sheep for which
the shepherd searches in the thorny wilderness. The
sheep has severed itself from the one who was its
guide; it has removed itself from the fold, gone its
own way and become lost. It is devoid of any
bearings and without homing instinct (see Luke
15:4-7).

At other times, Jesus pictured lost people as patients
whom the doctor gives up (Luke 5:31); worse, like
criminals on whom the sentence of death is carried
out (Matthew 13:40-42). He compares their lostness
to death (Luke 15:24), to destruction (Mark 12:9), to
damnation (John 5:28-29). Jesus thus presents lost
people as going astray and being condemned, lost in
such a way that it requires more than that they
simply be found—they must be awakened to eternal
life and saved.

The whole of Jesus' mission was to find lost people,
to rectify their sinful acts, to place them in the right
path. He came for this purpose. Jesus, the King of
Truth, taught that His mission to earth was "to seek
and to save what was lost" (Luke 19:10). Indeed, His
mission cannot be defined without speaking of
people as being lost.

Lost people are alienated from God. There can be
no doubt that Jesus had the same concept of lost

4

people as that set forth in Genesis 3 where, as one writer termed it, we find in embryo almost all the great doctrines about mankind's plight which appear in the remaining portions of the Bible: the divine explanation of the present ruined condition of our race, the subtle devices of our enemy the devil, our utter powerlessness to be righteous in own strength. Here we discover the spiritual effects of sin—our seeking to flee from God and our futile effort to cover our moral shame by devices of our own handiwork. Here, too, we discern the attitude of God toward the sinner.

Lost people practice wickedness and are wicked. By their sin Adam and Eve detached themselves from God. They became sinners. They and their posterity became full of sin—both the principles and acts of sin. "The Lord saw how great man's wickedness on the earth had become, and that every inclination of the thoughts of his heart was only evil all the time" (Genesis 6:5).

Two things are here laid to the charge of these sinful people. First, they practiced wickedness, great wickedness. We understand this to mean outward wickedness, for it is plainly distinguished from the wickedness of their hearts. They had made—and people continue to make—the earth a sink of sin, a stage on which they act out their wickedness in defiance of heaven. Second, "every inclination of the thoughts of [their] heart was only evil all the time." All their wicked practices are here traced to their fountainhead; corrupt hearts are the source of it all. People who had been created upright in all their faculties are now wholly disordered. Their hearts are the reverse of what they originally were. They are forges of evil imaginations, pools of inordinate affections, storehouses of all impiety. Whatever the "inclination of the thoughts"—whether judgments, choices, purposes, devices, desires—they are only evil, and continually so. Evil is ingrained in their hearts, interwoven in their very natures, sunk into the marrow of their souls.[3]

Lost people are totally depraved. Ever since Adam and Eve sinned in the Garden of Eden, the Bible presents people as totally corrupt—in their faculties, in the principles of their nature, in their understanding, in their will and in all their disposition and affections. Their heads and their hearts are totally depraved. All their senses—seeing, hearing, tasting, touching, smelling—are only instruments of sin and channels of corruption. Within them is nothing but sin and no good at all.

Both the prophet Isaiah and the apostle Paul confirm this assessment of mankind's condition:

> *Your whole head is injured,*
> * your whole heart afflicted.*
> *From the sole of your foot to the top of your*
> *   head*
> * there is no soundness.* Isaiah 1:5-6

> *All of us have become like one who is unclean,*
> * and all our righteous acts are like filthy rags.*
> Isaiah 64:6a

> *I know that nothing good lives in me, that is, in*
> *my sinful nature.* Romans 7:18a

> *The man without the Spirit does not accept the*
> *things that come from the Spirit of God, for*
> *they are foolishness to him.* 1 Corinthians 2:14

> *Those controlled by the sinful nature cannot*
> *please God.* Romans 8:8

> *There is no one who does good,*
> * not even one.* Romans 3:12b

These texts are indicative of a whole line of divine revelations about lost people which may be summed up in the Old Testament phrase:

*The heart is deceitful above all things
and beyond cure.* Jeremiah 17:9

The Bible does not mean to say there is no good in
people from the *human* point of view, but that there
is no good in people from *God's* point of view.
People in their natural state cannot satisfy God, for
He can require no less than perfection. As Thomas
Chalmers once said, "The righteousness of God is
that righteousness which His righteousness requires
Him to require." It is in this respect that "all have
sinned and fall short of the glory of God" (Romans
3:23).

**People "controlled by the sinful nature cannot
please God."** A comparison of Romans 8:8, just
quoted, with Romans 8:9 leads us to the conclusion
that being "controlled by the sinful nature" is the
opposite of being "controlled . . . by the Spirit." The
first results in sinfulness; the second results in
holiness. Sin, then, is a property of the sinful
nature—the human nature that was corrupted by the
fall of Adam and propagated from him to us, in that
corrupt state, by natural generation. Jesus called the
corrupt nature *flesh* because it is received by carnal
generation; and He called the new nature *spirit*
because it is received by spiritual generation: "Flesh
gives birth to flesh, but the Spirit gives birth to
spirit" (John 3:6). People unborn of the Spirit are still
and only in the flesh. And those who are in the
flesh—that is, controlled by the sinful
nature—cannot please God.

**By nature, lost people are "objects of wrath"
(Ephesians 2:3).** Those who are lost have not the
benefits of forgiveness for their sins or freedom from
condemnation. In their present state—the natural
state—God is against them.

**Lost people are "dead in [their] transgressions and
sins" (Ephesians 2:1).** They are not dying or mortal
or, yet again, condemned to death. They are

dead—now. People in their lost natural state not only lack the potential in themselves to be good, they are in fact dead. They can no more be brought to righteousness by the most vehement endeavors than a carcass can be brought to life by heat and rubbing. In one man, Adam, "sin entered the world, . . . and death through sin, and in this way death came to all men, because all sinned" (Romans 5:12).

Lost people follow "the ways of this world and of the ruler of the kingdom of the air, the spirit who is now at work in those who are disobedient" (Ephesians 2:2). "The ways of this world" describe the standard to which lost people in their natural state conform. "The ruler of the kingdom of the air" describes the master of all evil, the supreme ruler of the powers of wickedness—Satan himself—who rules those who are lost. The apostle John declares, "The whole world is under the control of the evil one" (1 John 5:19). And that "evil one" makes people disobedient. They are possessed by an obstinate opposition to the divine will. Disobedience is the very nature and essential character of those who are outside of Christ. They wholly belong to it.

People who are lost "fail the test" (2 Corinthians 13:5). Those who "fail the test" are rejected. Those lost outside of Christ—who do not have Christ within them—are rejected from partaking of God's salvation. The only test that satisfies God is Christ within. Without Him, people are lost, rejected.

People who are lost are "separate from Christ, . . . foreigners to the covenants of the promise, without hope and without God in the world" (Ephesians 2:12). These have no connection with Christ, no relation at all. They are strangers to God and to His covenant promises. They are not at home with God. They do not possess the rights and privileges of citizenship in God's kingdom and household. They are absolutely, utterly hopeless. Whether ignorant of or rejecting divine salvation as found in Jesus Christ, they have nothing to hope for beyond this world. They are immersed in darkness and misery. Being without God, they are without His help, His mercy, His protection.

The apostle Paul in a summation cites Old Testament Scriptures to prove the present lostness and corruption of all people outside of Christ:

> *What shall we conclude then? . . . Jews and*
> *Gentiles alike are all under sin. As it is written:*
>
> *"There is no one righteous, not even one;*
>   *there is no one who understands,*
>   *no one who seeks God.*
> *All have turned away,*
>   *they have together become worthless;*
> *there is no one who does good,*
>   *not even one."*
> *"Their throats are open graves;*
>   *their tongues practice deceit."*
> *"The poison of vipers is on their lips."*
>   *"Their mouths are full of cursing and*
>   *bitterness."*
> *"Their feet are swift to shed blood;*
>   *ruin and misery mark their ways,*
> *and the way of peace they do not know."*
>   *"There is no fear of God before their eyes."*
>   Romans 3:9-18

The lostness that Jesus, the King of Truth, taught and that Paul describes is already the state of those who are outside of Christ. It is so while they yet live. They are lost with reference to God. They have removed themselves far from the Father. They have been condemned by the Judge. Already they are out in the darkness, already hopelessly wandering and weighed down with judgment (John 3:18-20). And to save them, Jesus states, was the reason for His mission to earth (Luke 19:10).

9

III. The Intermediate State of People without Christ

What does "lostness" mean when unsaved people pass into the next world? What happens when a person, saved or not, dies?

Thankfully, we are not left to vague conjecture on this most important subject. The declarations of the Scriptures, especially the New Testament, are clear—sufficiently abundant and decisive. They lie everywhere upon the surface of the text, precisely designed to supplement the imperfect guesses and feeble hopes of a humanity that naturally longs to know what happens after death.

That the human soul survives the shock of death we can affirm on the authority of the Scriptures. Both Old and New Testament writers fully expected the conscious survival of the soul—apart from the body—after death. With positiveness and directness, Job, possibly the earliest of the Old Testament writers (Job 19:25–27) and the Psalmist (Psalm 17:15; 49:15), declare that the life of the soul does not die when the body dies.

> *I know that my Redeemer lives,*
>> *and that in the end he will stand upon the earth.*
> *And after my skin has been destroyed,*
>> *yet in my flesh I will see God;*
> *I myself will see him*
>> *with my own eyes. Job 19:25-27*

The frequent expressions, "gathered to his people" (Genesis 25:17; 35:29; 49:33) and "rested with his fathers" (1 Kings 11:43; 14:31) do not mean simply that the persons died, for the words are added to statements that properly express that idea. Neither do they mean that the persons were buried in the family cemetery, for this, too, is often stated specifically by the use of a different phrase. The expressions signified to the Hebrews a reunion with their forefathers in the other world, or, as David tenderly expresses it with regard to his deceased child, "I will go to him" (2 Samuel 12:23). The writer of Ecclesiastes, in referring to death, adds, "And the spirit returns to God who gave it" (Ecclesiastes 12:7)—further biblical corroboration of the survival of the human soul after death.[4]

Jesus' account of the rich man and Lazarus (Luke 16:19-31) is also legitimate and essential to our understanding of what occurs immediately upon death. Note that:

> Consciousness will continue after death, together with memory and the same instincts and sentiments as characterize people during the present life.

> The good will be happy and the wicked miserable, and both from a recognition of their true character and what they deserved.

> They will be aware of others' final destinies, as well as their own.

> There is no means or possibility of a transition from the condition of the lost to that of the blessed.

> All further efforts on the part of God for salvation after death are abandoned.[5]

Jesus said to the penitent thief dying beside Him at Calvary, "Today you will be with me in paradise" (Luke 23:43). Paul anticipated his own death as "be[ing] with Christ" (Philippians 1:23). The writer to the Hebrews saw in "Mount Zion, . . . the heavenly Jerusalem," not only an innumerable company of angels "in joyful assembly," but "the church of the firstborn, whose names are written in heaven," and "the spirits of righteous men made perfect" (Hebrews 12:22-23).

From these Bible references, by no means exhaustive, we can be certain that the soul will be conscious in the disembodied state. The faculties that constitute or belong to the soul—thought, memory, feeling, imagination—will remain after death, unaltered and unimpaired in their nature. We are also warranted in saying that during this interim period, pending the reunion of soul and body, the saved will be occupied with unalloyed delights of a spiritual nature.

Those, however, destined to everlasting condemnation will suffer misery. As if their present incarceration in the agony of hell's fire was insufficient, they suffer the suspense of their anticipated eternal doom. They are like criminals in the interval between conviction and execution. Theirs is the "fearful expectation of judgment and of raging fire that will consume the enemies of God" (Hebrews 10:27).

Article 40 of the Church of England, adopted during the 16th century reign of Edward VI, states the case briefly and clearly:

> The souls of them that depart this life do neither die with the bodies nor sleep idly. They which say that the souls of such as depart hence do sleep, being without all sense, feeling, or perceiving, until the day of judgment . . . do utterly dissent from the right belief declared to us in Holy Scripture.

The Bible does not give us further detailed information about the intermediate state of either the lost or the saved. This, no doubt, is due to the tentative, temporary nature of this intermediate state. The sacred writers prefer to hasten on to the

12

resurrection state—mankind's final and eternal condition.

IV. The Resurrection State of People without Christ

The Bible teaches that all the human denizens of earth will be resurrected, irrespective of their moral qualities or their final doom. Jesus declared:

> *A time is coming when all who are in their graves will hear [the Son of God's] voice and come out—those who have done good will rise to live, and those who have done evil will rise to be condemned.* John 5:29

The apostle Paul expressed before Felix, the Roman governor, the universal Jewish expectation "that there will be a resurrection of both the righteous and the wicked" (Acts 24:15).

Even Christians have an incomplete, inadequate understanding of the resurrected body itself and its relation to the soul by which it is forever to be inhabited. A sufficient explanation, therefore, is essential.

Resurrection is from the Latin "re," meaning *again,* and "surgere," *to rise;* thus, "to rise again." The dictionary defines resurrection as the fresh bringing forth of the selfsame thing that was before. Paul spoke of it this way: "He who raised Christ from the dead will also give life to your mortal bodies through his Spirit" (Romans 5:11).

If, then, the body that died does not rise again, as some maintain, we shall have to relinquish the word *resurrection* and find some other word to explain what does happen. But the church from its beginning has consistently held to the unaltered meaning of *resurrection.* From the days of the apostles, without a missing link, the unbroken

13

testimony of the church creeds maintain that the human body that died is the body that will be raised. Note:

The Apostles' Creed

(Previous to A.D. 600) ". . . and the resurrection of the flesh."

(As it now reads) ". . . the resurrection of the body, and the life everlasting."

The Athanasian Creed

(5th century—accepted by the Greek, Roman and English churches) ". . . at whose coming all men shall rise again with their bodies, and shall render an account of their own works."

The Scots Confession

(Adopted A.D. 1560 and Part I of the Constitution of the United Presbyterian Church in the U.S.A.) "In the general judgment there shall be given to every man and woman resurrection of the flesh. The sea shall give up her dead; the earth, those that are buried within her. Yea, the Eternal, our God, shall stretch out His hand on the dust, and the dead shall arise incorruptible, and in the very substance of the self-same flesh that every man now bears, to receive, according to their works, glory or punishment."

The Belgic Confession

(A.D. 1561) "For all the dead shall be raised out of the earth, and their souls joined and united with their proper bodies in which they formerly lived. As for those who then shall be living, they shall not die as the others, but be changed in the twinkling of an eye, and from corruptible become incorruptible."

Confession of the Eastern Church

(A.D. 1643. Greek and Russian Orthodox churches) "There will be a resurrection of human bodies, alike of the righteous and the wicked, from the death that has passed upon them. . . . They shall be altogether the same bodies with which they lived in this world."

The Heidelberg Catechism

(A.D. 1563. German Reformed church and Part I of the Constitution of the United Presbyterian Church in the U.S.A.) "Question: What comfort does the resurrection of the body afford thee? Answer: That not only my soul, after this life, shall be immediately taken up to Christ its Head, but also that this my body, raised by the power of Christ, shall again be united with my soul and made like unto the glorious body of Christ."

The Westminster Confession

(A.D. 1647. All Presbyterian churches) "At the last day such as are found alive shall not die, but be changed; and all the dead shall be raised up with the self-same bodies and none other, although with different qualities, which shall be united again to their souls forever."

In the ultimate, however, the proof that all people will be resurrected is not in the dictionary meaning of *resurrected* or the testimony of the church creeds, but in the resurrection of Jesus Christ. The biblical argument is that Christ predicted His own resurrection and actually arose in the manner He said He would. He thus proved both His power to do as He said and His veracity in all His declarations. And He has further promised that He will raise up at the last day all that are in their graves. Not only is Jesus' own resurrection proof of His power to raise the dead, but it becomes the model of what we may expect when our bodies are resurrected. We therefore examine Jesus' resurrection and, as well, His resurrection body.

On the day of Pentecost the apostle Peter said of Jesus whom the Jews had crucified, "God has raised this Jesus to life, and we are all witnesses of the fact" (Acts 2:32). If Christ had been completely changed after His resurrection, the apostles could not have recognized or identified Him. Thus they could not have been witnesses to His resurrection. It was necessary that Christ should be recognized, and that so unmistakably that His previous predictions might be established and Christianity proved true.

Christ's resurrection was at once the testing point and crowning evidence both of His Sonship and His Messiahship. Unless His resurrection had been completely proved, Christianity must have failed. As Paul would later put it, "If Christ has not been raised, our preaching is useless and so is your faith. . . . You are still in your sins" (1 Corinthians 15:14, 17). Recognition, then, is not a trivial matter. Had the disciples and others not recognized the risen Jesus, they could not have testified to His resurrection; ultimately, they would have been forced to deny that He rose from the dead.

Accordingly, we find Christ affording to all His disciples the fullest possible evidence that He was still the same Jesus they had known before His crucifixion. In many ways He proved indubitably that He had undergone no essential change. By His voice, by his hands and feet pierced by the nails, by the spear wound in His side, by His eating food in the presence of His disciples, letting them touch and feel his "flesh and bones," Jesus convinced them all that He was indeed the same Jesus whom they had known and not an apparition.

All of the external marks and traits of Christ's resurrection body substantially agreed with the body that was put in the tomb. "Look at my hands and my feet," Jesus said to His disciples, likely drawing their attention to the nail wounds. "It is I myself! Touch me and see; a ghost does not have flesh and bones, as you see I have" (Luke 24:39). Jesus' resurrection body corresponded in minute detail with His preresurrection body.

All of this is in exact accord with what we are directly told in Scripture as to the kind of resurrection body all of us will have. There is every reason to believe, both from revelation and the nature of the case, that for both the just and the unjust the same body that died will come forth in the resurrection. At that time the soul will return to inhabit the same body it was in before death.

About the post-resurrection state of the lost the Bible discloses considerable information. And it is enough to cause us to shudder with horror.

In their resurrection bodies the lost will be judged. "Man is destined to die once, and after that to face judgment" (Hebrews 9:27). Concerning them, the sentence has already been promulgated: "Let him who does wrong continue to do wrong; let him who is vile continue to be vile" (Revelation 22:11).

The lost will be punished in hell. The English word *hell* is used to translate three words found in the Greek language of the original New Testament: Hades, the place of the unregenerate dead; Gehenna, the post-resurrection place of their punishment; and Tartarus, the deepest abyss of Hades. Writes Herbert Lockyer:

> In the word *Gehenna,* occurring 12 times in the New Testament, 11 of which are in the first three Gospels, we come across a picture word having an historic origin. It is a shortened term for the Vale of Hinnom—Ge-Hinnom—a valley south of

Jerusalem. The story of this place is told in Second Chronicles 28:3.

In earlier days it was a fair garden, but under two kings became a place of idolatry. Little children were placed within a heated metal image, thus being made to pass through the fire as an act of worship. In good King Josiah's time, he abolished this repulsive and cruel form of idolatry and defiled the Vale of Hinnom by making it the great rubbish-heap of Jerusalem. Dead animals, unburied bodies of criminals were consumed therein. Fires continually burned with an intense burning on that immense pile. It was still used that way in our Lord's day.

Now this word *Gehenna* is clearly used by Christ as the name for the place of punishment of wicked men (Matthew 5:22, 29, 30; 10:28; 18:9; 23:15, 33). In His use of it He did not mean the Gehenna burning outside the Jerusalem walls, but used it as a symbol of utter ruin. It means consignment to something equivalent to the great rubbish-heap of Gehenna.[6]

The lost will suffer in hell in their bodies. The bodies of the lost that are laid in the ground shall be raised again in order that the same body that sinned on earth shall suffer in the hereafter. It is neither logical nor biblical that the body that sinned here should be replaced by another body to suffer in hell for that sin. The body that was the soul's companion in sin on earth should not lie forever in the dust while another body, that took no part in the sinning, should be the soul's companion in torment.

Then, too, since the Savior Himself will forever bear the marks of the conflict through which He passed on the cross, would it not be unreasonable and unjust for the ungodly not to everlastingly bear the *stigmata* of their abuse of their bodies? Further, since they would have none of Christ and His saving benefits in this life, should they expect to have any of His redemptive benefits for their bodies in the resurrection life to come? If, therefore, the bodies of the righteous will be glorious, then those of the wicked will be repulsive.

Indeed, the profligate, the drunkards, the debauchees will bear a natural penalty in their bodies no less than a moral penalty in their souls. Those tongues that in this life were employed in mocking religion, in cursing and swearing, in lying, backbiting and boasting will long for water to assuage the eternal flames (Luke 16:24). The same feet that stood in the way of sinners and carried them in their ungodly activities shall stand in the burning lake (Mark 9:45). And the same covetous and lascivious eyes shall smart from the smoke of the pit. The ears which refused to hear sermons or seasonable exhortations, admonitions and reproofs will hear the abundant weeping and wailing and gnashing of teeth (Luke 16:27–31; Matthew 24:30). They will suffer in their bodies—not ethereal, gaseous bodies, but solid bodies of flesh and bone.

The lost will continue to sin in their resurrection bodies. When Satan was cast out of heaven, he manifested his intense hatred of God and eventually his vehement malice toward mankind by seducing our first parents and destroying the world. Peter informs us that since that time, "the devil prowls around like a roaring lion looking for someone to devour" (1 Peter 5:8). John declares that the same malignant being "leads the whole world astray" (Revelation 12:9). What a dreadful picture the Bible paints of this evil, hungry being, roaring with rage, going about to devour rational, immortal people throughout the earth.

It is plain that the evil desires of Satan are not diminished by his banishment and sufferings. On this account it is reasonable to believe that all other evil beings will sustain in the next world the same character, the same desires and the same practices that caused their banishment.

That the lost will continue their sin in the next world is attested to in Revelation 22:15: "Outside are the dogs, those who practice magic arts, the sexually immoral, the murderers, the idolaters and everyone who loves and practices falsehood." These sinful drives of the lost will be exceedingly powerful and unrestrained.

The lost have no options; their state and condition as sinners is fixed. For them there will be no alternative. "No sacrifice for sins is left, but only a fearful expectation of judgment and of raging fire that will consume the enemies of God" (Hebrews 10:26-27). God has already offered His ultimate Atonement; what further provision could He possibly make?

The lost will suffer forever. Jesus Himself describes hell (Gehenna) as the place "where the fire never goes out" (Mark 9:43).

In several places (for example, Daniel 12:2, Matthew 3:12; 13:36-43) the Bible sets forth the happiness of the righteous and the sufferings of the wicked in what may be called a parallel manner. No intimation is given that the duration of one will not be equal with that of the other. The words *eternal, everlasting, forever* as employed in the New Testament refuse to be despoiled of their content by linguistic analysis. As used by the Savior and the apostles, they are to be taken at face value. Thus they convey an intelligible and reliable, however awful, truth concerning the duration of the impenitents' punishment. If heaven is unending, so is hell, for the words are applied to both in the same manner and without any hint of a distinction in their use.

The doom of the lost is inescapable. To the rich man in hell Abraham said, "Between us and you a great chasm has been fixed, so that those who want to go from here to you cannot, nor can anyone cross over from there to us" (Luke 16:26). Mercy will not be extended, leniency will not be offered, amnesty will not be declared, paroles will not be issued. Over the entrance of hell stands the inscription, "Abandon Hope All You Who Enter Here."

Those who die outside of Christ will suffer irremedial loss. They will have lost forever the grace of God—His unmerited favor and proffered mercy. They will be irretrievably gone and that forever.

The unsaved will never hear another gospel message. Church, the prayers of Christians, the stirring hymns will be past. Godly parents, children, husband or wife will be missed, their company and faces never to be enjoyed again. The lost might have had a haven of rest; they exchanged it for an everlasting lake of fire and an abode of woe. They might have had glorified bodies; in their place are unredeemed bodies full of sin, corruption, disease and filth. They might have mingled with the saints in the celestial Jerusalem; instead they mingle with beings filled with every imaginable evil. They had opportunity to be children of the heavenly King; they are now vessels of wrath fit only for eternal torments.

It must not be overlooked that this irremedial loss is the unsaved's own deliberate and continued choice personally and freely made. It is, in fact, not so much an infliction of punishment as a withholding of that which could not be received, or if received would be a compulsory bestowal—an act of tyranny. The situation of the lost will be truly of a piece with all their previous conduct and chosen pursuits. Their condition in the future state has all along been in their own hands, freely determined by themselves. The question, therefore, is not what God imposes on them in the next life but what they—by disposition, character and nature—take into it. They carry *themselves* into it; they can take nothing else with them there. The penalty is inherent in the pride, envy, selfishness and all evil passion which continue in the surviving, rejoined soul and body. Their enormous losses in hell are but God's ratification of their decisive choices in this life.

V. What about Those Who Have Not Heard of Jesus?

Almost all biblically centered Christians accept the justice of punishment meted out to gospel-hardened people who have ignored or obstinately rejected Christ's offer of salvation. But what about those who by geographic or historical accident live in cultures where Jesus is unknown? What about those who, although they may have a rudimentary knowledge of Jesus, have never been meaningfully evangelized? Is it fair that they should be in unspeakable torture forever? May there not be in the depth of the divine mercy opportunity for them in the future state?

There are those who have concluded that all such will be saved. They have substantiated their views, however, not by a contextual interpretation of all relevant Scripture but rather by fashioning their concepts of God's love, justice and morality after their own. Sometimes they have reasoned from assumptions that have no biblical support. They have resorted to human feelings, human sentiments, human intuitions. Where they have appealed to the Bible, it is to isolated "proof-texts" that only seem to confirm their wishful speculations.

The answer to this heart-rending question must come not from human reasoning and human sympathy, but from Jesus Christ and the Scriptures.

22

What did the omniscient, holy Jesus teach? What do the Christ-authenticated Scriptures say? Any response not anchored in this bedrock of Bible truth has no more authority than the person who proposes it.

Jesus said:

> *I am the gate; whoever enters through me will be saved.* John 10:9

> *I am the way. . . . No one comes to the Father except through me.* John 14:6

> *I tell you the truth, no one can see the kingdom of God unless he is born again.* John 3:3

Jesus declared Himself to be the only door and the only road to the Father. He has not opened a variety of ways to be saved. There are no optional alternatives. For a person to qualify for heaven, Jesus makes regeneration, that is, a spiritual rebirth, absolutely necessary.

The apostle Peter declared of Jesus, "Salvation is found in no one else, for there is no other name under heaven given to men by which we must be saved" (Acts 4:12). It is not a question of whether there "is good in other religions"; it is a matter of there being but one divinely appointed way of salvation. All who miss this one way of salvation are in peril.

The apostle Paul is equally unbending. To those in Colossae who had put their trust in Jesus Christ he wrote that God the Father "has qualified you to share in the inheritance of the saints in the kingdom of light." He adds, "For he has rescued us from the dominion of darkness and brought us into the kingdom of the Son he loves, in whom we have redemption, the forgiveness of sins" (Colossians 1:12-14). It is clear that those who go to heaven are they who qualify, and qualification is through Christ, who alone forgives sins.

Paul has this to say about the effects of sin and its only remedy: "The wages of sin is death, but the gift of God is eternal life in Christ Jesus our Lord" (Romans 6:23). William G.T. Shedd comments:

> Sin is the suicidal action of the human will. A man is not forced to kill himself, but if he does, he cannot bring himself to life again. And a man is not forced to sin, but if he does, he cannot get back to where he was before sinning. He cannot get back to innocency nor can he get back to holiness of heart.[7]

In the early paragraphs of his letter to the Romans, Paul argues that all people outside of Christ are in such a situation:

> *The wrath of God is being revealed from heaven against all the godlessness and wickedness of men who suppress the truth by their wickedness, since what may be known about God is plain to them, because God has made it plain to them. For since the creation of the world God's invisible qualities—his eternal power and divine nature—have been clearly seen, being understood from what has been made, so that men are without excuse.*
> Romans 1:18-20

Citing Old Testament Scriptures,[8] Paul concludes:

> *There is no one righteous, not even one;*
>   *there is no one who understands,*
>   *no one who seeks God.*
> *All have turned away,*
>   *they have together become worthless;*
> *there is no one who does good,*
>   *not even one.* Romans 3:10-12

Pagans who have never heard of the true God and His Son Jesus Christ, Gentile moralists, Jewish legalists—whose case Paul has just taken up (see Romans 2:17-29)—all alike are under sin's power and sin's lethal remuneration and thus unable to achieve eternal life by any efforts of their own. They are all under God's judgment. The remedy—the *only* remedy God has revealed—is Jesus Christ, the Giver of eternal life.

For all members of the human family, the alternatives are two: eternal life and eternal death. There is no neutral territory between these two immeasurable destinies. The Bible makes these affirmations of all persons, whether they have heard of Christ or not.

It is hardly necessary to multiply quotations. This sense that salvation is only in Jesus and that people—whatever their status—are saved only by a conscious surrender to Him runs through the whole of the New Testament. In no place and on no account is it ever modified or set aside.

The wondrous fact of the gospel is that "everyone who calls on the name of the Lord will be saved" (Romans 10:13). But the Scriptures ask, "How, then, can they call on the one they have not believed in? And how can they believe in the one of whom they have not heard? And how can they hear without someone preaching to them?" (Romans 10:14).

Devastating logic! God has ordained that people should be saved through the preaching of the gospel. And Jesus has commanded us to preach it to all people (Luke 24:47). There is not a word in God's Book that so much as intimates He saves human beings without using human agents to take the good news of salvation to them. Nothing in the Scriptures implies that God in His sovereignty and great love, will wink at the guilt of those who had no opportunity to know of Christ Jesus.

J. Herbert Kane puts the whole matter correctly and succinctly in his book, *Christian Missions in Biblical Perspective*:

> To say, "God will take care of the heathen," and leave it there is to close one's eyes to the clear statements of the Bible and the hard, cold facts of history. The question is not whether God will take care of the heathen, but *how* He does it. He has made it abundantly clear in His Word that it is His will and purpose to care for the heathen *through the Church*. The *miracle* of reconciliation was accomplished by the death and resurrection of Christ. The *ministry* of reconciliation has been committed to the church. If the church for any reason fails to fulfill its God-given ministry, the church, and not God, must bear the blame. World evangelization *can* be achieved by human means and manpower. It is both futile and foolish to expect God to achieve by supernatural means what the church can accomplish by human means.[9]

In one of his most haunting missionary songs, A.B. Simpson, 19th century founder of The Christian and Missionary Alliance, asks:

> O Church of Christ, what wilt thou say
> When, in the awful judgment day,
>   They charge thee with their doom?[10]

VI. Conclusion

I have attempted to look at the biblical meaning of "lostness" as it relates to the unconverted in their present condition, their intermediate situation at death and their final state in the resurrection at the last day.

When the unconverted die, their souls go out into immediate and conscious suffering. At the resurrection, their unredeemed bodies will be raised from the grave and reunited with their unregenerate and tormented souls. And all of those thus resurrected will be confined to a region where there is no hope, no end, and no morally upright beings to hold the balance against evil. It is a place where nothing good can follow them—no holy beauty; no virgin innocency; no guiltless, guileless love of parents, spouse, child, brother, friend. It is a place of no virtue, no decency ever, none of the decorum here that at least serves to make vice less hideous. It is a place where there is no restraining providence of God—no interference by God at all.

Hell will be a congregation of the unsaved, in the unregenerate state in which they died, driven together into one settlement. There all the cruel acts of men will be played out remorselessly. Cannibals, headhunters, rapists, murderers, dope fiends, sodomites, rioters, the lawless, liars and all the other varieties of unsaved men and women will be there. Added to that will be the tormenting demons, the unquenchable fire and the continual weeping and wailing and gnashing of teeth. In that place and condition they will exist forever.

This certain, terrifying and eternal condition of the lost is a vital and powerful motivation for evangelism.

ENDNOTES

1. Kenneth B. Kantzer, *The Church's Worldwide Mission* (Waco, Texas: Word Books, 1966), pp. 30-31.

2. William G.T. Shedd, *Dogmatic Theology*, Vol. 2 (Nashville, Tennessee: Thomas Nelson, 1980 reprint), pp. 675, 680.

3. Thomas Boston, *Human Nature in its Fourfold State* (London: The Banner of Truth Trust, 1964), pp. 60-61.

4. James Strong, *The Doctrine of a Future Life* (New York: Eaton and Mains, 1891), pp. 37-51.

5. *Ibid.*, pp. 58-59.

6. Herbert Lockyer, *The Immortality of Saints* (London: Pickering & Inglis, Ltd., n.d.), pp. 109-110.

7. William G.T. Shedd, *The Doctrine of Endless Punishment* (Minneapolis, Minnesota: Klock & Klock, 1980 reprint), p. 149.

8. Psalm 14:1-3; 53:1-3; Ecclesiastes 7:20.

9. J. Herbert Kane, *Christian Missions in Biblical Perspective* (Grand Rapids, Michigan: Baker Book House, 1976), p. 300.

10. Albert B. Simpson, "A Missionary Cry," *Hymns of the Christian Life* (Camp Hill, Pennsylvania: Christian Publications, 1978), p. 462.

BIBLIOGRAPHY

Boston, Thomas. *Human Nature in its Four Fold State*. London: The Banner of Truth and Trust, 1964 reprint.

Cooke, R.J. *Doctrine of the Resurrection*. New York: Phillips & Hunt, 1884.

Kane, J. Herbert. *Christian Missions in Biblical Perspective*. Grand Rapids, Michigan: Baker Book House, 1976.

Killen, J.M. *Our Friends in Heaven*. Cincinnati, Ohio: Far Western Book Concern of M.E. Church, 1857.

Kittel, G., ed. *Theological Dictionary of the New Testament*. Grand Rapids, Michigan: Eerdmans, 1968.

Lockyer, Herbert. *The Immortality of Saints*. London: Pickering & Inglis, Ltd., n.d.

Merrill, S.M. *The New Testament Idea of Hell*. New York: Phillips & Hunt, 1878.

Salmond, S.D.F. *Christian Doctrine of Immortaility*. Edinburgh: T. & T. Clark, 1897.

Scroggie, W. Graham. *What about Heaven?* London: Pickering & Inglis, n.d.

Shedd, William G.T. *The Doctrine of Endless Punishment*. Minneapolis, Minnesota: Klock & Klock, 1980 reprint.

Strong, James. *The Doctrine of a Future Life*. New York: Eaton & Mains, 1891.